Europrivacy™/®

The first European Data Protection Seal

Europrivacy™/®

The first European Data Protection Seal

ALICE TURLEY

IT Governance Publishing

Every possible effort has been made to ensure that the information in this book is accurate at the time of going to press, and the publishers and the authors cannot accept responsibility for any errors or omissions, however caused. Any opinions expressed in this book are those of the authors, not the publisher. Websites identified are for reference only, not endorsement, and any website visits are at the reader's own risk. No responsibility for loss or damage occasioned to any person acting, or refraining from action, as a result of the material in this publication can be accepted by the publisher or the authors.

Apart from any fair dealing for the purposes of research or private study, or criticism or review, as permitted under the Copyright, Designs and Patents Act 1988, this publication may only be reproduced, stored or transmitted, in any form, or by any means, with the prior permission in writing of the publisher or, in the case of reprographic reproduction, in accordance with the terms of licences issued by the Copyright Licensing Agency. Enquiries concerning reproduction outside those terms should be sent to the publishers at the following address:

IT Governance Publishing Ltd
Unit 3, Clive Court
Bartholomew's Walk
Cambridgeshire Business Park
Ely, Cambridgeshire
CB7 4EA
United Kingdom
www.itgovernancepublishing.co.uk

The author has asserted the rights of the author under the Copyright, Designs and Patents Act, 1988, to be identified as the author of this work.

First published in the United Kingdom in 2024 by IT Governance Publishing.

ISBN 978-1-78778-515-1

Cover image originally sourced from Shutterstock®.

ABOUT THE AUTHOR

Alice Turley is a knowledgeable and experienced senior governance, risk, compliance and privacy consultant with IT Governance Europe Ltd (*www.itgovernance.eu*). She is also a qualified data privacy, information security, risk and compliance professional, consultant and trainer, and a Payment Card Industry Data Security Standard Qualified Security Assessor (PCI DSS QSA). She is highly experienced in providing expert and solution-based advice, skilled in developing compliance, privacy and risk frameworks and assessing risk, as well as developing and executing monitoring and auditing programmes, and an expert in implementing and auditing ISO/IEC and BS standards.

Alice has provided consultancy on privacy information management and information security management systems across a wide range of industries in both the private and public sectors, and is a certified Europrivacy™/® Lead Implementor and Lead Auditor.

CONTENTS

CHAPTER 1: WHAT IS EUROPRIVACY?

On 12 October 2022, the European Data Protection Board (EDPB) endorsed the Europrivacy certification scheme. This is the first certification mechanism, or data protection seal, that entities can achieve to demonstrate their compliance with the General Data Protection Regulation (GDPR) and other national data privacy obligations.

The certification scheme has been developed through the European research programme and is maintained by the European Centre for Certification and Privacy (ECCP), which is referred to as the scheme owner.

The Europrivacy scheme is based on certifying processing activities. This means that certification is awarded at a data processing activity level as opposed to the entity as a whole. Europrivacy recommends that the initial certification commences with at least two processing activities, extending the certification to include more data processing with time. However, an entity can initially certify to one, or more than two, processing activities. The processing activities being assessed for Europrivacy compliance are documented within the entity's Target of Evaluation (ToE): a report that is not dissimilar to a scope statement under ISO 27001.

The Europrivacy scheme embraces a broad range of data processing operations, including new technologies such as blockchain, Internet of Things, automated cars, smart cities and artificial intelligence, and is suitable for both data controllers and data processors.

1: What is Europrivacy?

Europrivacy was developed in adherence with ISO/IEC 17065 and ISO/IEC 17021-1 in addition to Articles 42 and 43 (pertaining to requirements for certification and certification bodies) of the GDPR.

CHAPTER 2: BENEFITS/ADVANTAGES OF EUROPRIVACY CERTIFICATION

There are considerable advantages for entities that certify some, or all, of their personal data processing activities to Europrivacy:

- The GDPR mentions the requirement to implement appropriate technical and organisational measures to protect personal data and the processing of personal data 18 times. However, it does not provide a framework to specify what appropriate technical and organisational measures could actually look like, which has left a gap for entities to fill.
  Europrivacy provides a detailed framework of appropriate technical and organisational measures that an entity can use to assess, validate and demonstrate the compliance of their data processing activities. The Europrivacy checks and controls can be used across a wide range of data processing operations, including distinct ones such as new technologies, online services and the health sector, to help reduce the financial, and legal, risks that an entity is exposed to.
- Certification confirming GDPR compliance will demonstrate to that entity's customers, clients, employees, suppliers and other stakeholders that protection of personal data that it is processing is of utmost importance. Certification can be used to

provide assurance to data subjects and all the entity's stakeholders that the entity is adequately processing their personal data, and adhering to the rights and freedoms of data subjects.

- Non-compliance with the requirements of the GDPR could lead to fines of up to €20 million or 4% of total worldwide turnover, whichever is greater, so adhering to the Europrivacy scheme is only going to reduce the financial and legal risks of nonconformity.
- The Europrivacy checks and controls can also be used as a due diligence tool for selecting and assessing data processors. By requiring data processors to become certified, the entity will minimise the level of due diligence that needs to be carried out before onboarding or renewing a data processor and reduce the risks that are inherent within the data controller/data processor relationship.
- Entities in non-EU jurisdictions that provide goods or services into the EU or that monitor the behaviour of data subjects in the EU can certify their processing activities to Europrivacy to demonstrate compliance with their GDPR obligations. This provides reassurance to data subjects, and builds trust and confidence with other stakeholders. This, in turn, can provide an entity with a competitive advantage and improve its reputation.
- From the outset of the Europrivacy certification journey, entities can access comprehensive resources

and tools on the online, active Europrivacy community. These include certification scheme documentation, complementary national and domain-specific criteria, answers to frequently asked questions, a library of guidance, documentation templates and national obligations, useful links and discussion forums.

- The Europrivacy checks and controls are continually updated to take into account any regulatory or legislative changes, advice and guidance from the EDPB, and changes to national and domain-specific obligations.
- Similar to the ISO standards, Europrivacy certification is a three-year certification process, with an annual surveillance audit carried out by an independent certification body. This certification body must be approved by the relevant data protection supervisory authority/authorities to conduct Europrivacy certification, surveillance and recertification audits.

CHAPTER 3: PREPARATION FOR THE CERTIFICATION PROCESS

An entity (applicant) can apply for Europrivacy certification either via the Europrivacy website[1], where they will be matched with a consulting company, or directly to a consulting company. It is important to note that an applicant cannot use any consulting company – they must use one that is deemed Europrivacy qualified. Europrivacy maintains a list of qualified consulting companies[2] on its website, which is available for anyone to view.

When an applicant contacts a qualified consulting company, the consulting company will prepare a Europrivacy welcome offer explaining the services to be provided and the costs involved. Once the applicant accepts this offer, the agreement is considered validated and the consulting company will start the implementation process by activating the Europrivacy Welcome Pack for the applicant's data protection officer (DPO).

The Europrivacy Welcome Pack is offered by Europrivacy to all applicants and consists of:

- An introductory Europrivacy training course for the DPO;

---

[1] *www.europrivacy.org*.

[2] *www.europrivacy.org/en/partners/list*.

- Access to the online tools and resources on the Europrivacy Community website during the three years of certification;
- The Europrivacy certificate publication fees (for three years) on the official registry of Europrivacy certificates;
- A privacy pack registration; and
- Access to the Europrivacy Flash Alerts with the latest regulatory and criteria updates during the three years.

The welcome pack can be purchased directly from Europrivacy or from the qualified consulting company, usually at a slightly discounted price.

Europrivacy certification requires an applicant to have a DPO in place – this can be an internal appointment, or an external entity that provides DPO as a service facilities. Regardless of whether the DPO is internal or external, the person must complete the DPO statement template that is provided by Europrivacy.

The next step in preparing for certification is to determine the data processing activity that is to be certified. While an applicant can specify one or more data processing activities, Europrivacy recommends selecting two priority data processing activities for the initial certification. The consulting company works with the applicant to select the most appropriate data processing activities. Once the data processing activities have been selected, the consulting company will help the applicant complete the Europrivacy certification application form and specify the ToE. The ToE specifies the processing activities to be certified and can list a number of personal data processing activities. It is crucial that the ToE specifies and delimits the scope of each personal data processing activity included for certification. The ToE must:

- Describe the data processing activity that is within the scope of certification;
- Demonstrate the data flows in a diagram, e.g. a data flow map, including showing where the data processing activity commences and ends;
- Distinguish the types of data being processed;
- Provide a detailed description of all operations and systems relating to the data processing activities within scope of certification, including any relevant assurance controls; and
- Outline any interfaces of the data processing with other processing operations.

At this stage, it is important for the consulting company to determine how ready the applicant is for certification and what tasks need to be completed. Therefore, the consulting company normally performs a gap analysis to assess the applicant's compliance with all the Europrivacy criteria, checks and controls, and to identify all actions that need to be taken.

Following the gap analysis, the consulting company will prepare all required documentation that the applicant will need, not just for their certification process, but also to implement an effective data protection management system. The consulting company will refer to the Europrivacy policy and procedures checklist in addition to the Europrivacy documentation checklist, both of which have been created and provided by Europrivacy.

While the consulting company will help the applicant prepare the majority of the documentation required for Europrivacy certification, the National Obligations Conformity Assessment Report (NOCAR) must be completed by a person who has expertise and qualifications in law and data protection regulations. It must also be completed with due diligence, professionalism and objectivity, and by a person other than the DPO to ensure that a conflict of interest does not exist.

Next, we have a key step: assessing the compliance of the ToE with all the Europrivacy criteria, checks and controls (the Europrivacy criteria are discussed in more detail in the next section). The consulting company will complete this compliance assessment, sometimes referred to as a readiness assessment or an internal audit, and communicate all identified nonconformities to the applicant.

The applicant must take steps to implement controls to resolve all identified nonconformities, and the consulting company must subsequently check each nonconformity to validate that all have been successfully remediated.

It is at this stage that the consulting company will invite the applicant to select a certification body; as previously noted, it must be a Europrivacy qualified certification body, which can be found on the list of official partners on the Europrivacy website.[3] The applicant then completes an application form (with the assistance of the consulting

---

[3] *www.europrivacy.org/en/partners/list*.

company) and submits this to the selected certification body.

The consulting company will support the applicant during the certification process. The stages involved in this process are outlined in the Certification Process section of the book.

CHAPTER 4: THE EUROPRIVACY CERTIFICATION CRITERIA

Europrivacy has specified detailed lists of criteria, checks and controls – these lists are maintained by the ECCP (the scheme owner) and are provided to consulting companies and applicants in Excel and Word templates via the Europrivacy Community online forum.

The lists are also used by the certification bodies for assessing compliance, and each criteria, check and control must be documented by the applicant (with the consulting company's help) with the evidence to demonstrate compliance fully documented.

Currently, there are three Europrivacy certification criteria categories. However, it could be argued that complying with national requirements is a fourth criteria category, so it has been included in the list below:

1. GDPR core criteria.
2. Complementary contextual checks and controls.
3. Technical and organisational checks and controls.
4. National requirements.

Each of these will now be discussed in more detail.

1. GDPR core criteria

The GDPR core criteria are focused on the key requirements of the GDPR articles. An applicant must be able to demonstrate their compliance with each of these requirements. It should be noted that compliance with the GDPR core criteria is mandatory for all certifications.

On the GDPR Core Criteria checklist, there are ten core criteria categories, each with a number of sub-requirements. Each criteria requirement has a reference ID; a section to input as to whether the control is applicable to data controllers, data processors or both; a section to note if the control is specific to a data processing activity or common to several data processing activities; a section to note if the control is mandatory, not required for simple data processing but mandatory for high-risk data processing, contextual or exempt; a title; the criteria/requirement; implementation guidance; suggested means of verification; and the related GDPR article number.

The ten GDPR core criteria categories are as follows:

Core Criteria 1: Lawfulness of data processing

It is no surprise that having a lawful basis for processing personal data is the first of the core criteria. Article 5.1(a) of the GDPR states that personal data must be processed lawfully, fairly and in a transparent manner. To ensure that the lawful aspect of this data protection principle is being addressed, an entity must only process personal data if it has a lawful basis to do so. But it cannot be any lawful basis; it must be at least one of the six lawful bases documented under Article 6.1 of the GDPR.

The six lawful bases[4] are:

---

[4] Article 6.1 of the GDPR.

i. The data subject has given their consent to the processing of their personal data. It is important to note that consent is one of the lawful bases – just because it is listed first, an entity should not fall into the trap of believing it is the most important. There are five other lawful bases that an entity may well be able, and in fact it may be easier, to use. However, if an applicant is processing personal data based on the lawful basis of consent, then they must ensure that this consent is freely given, specific, informed and communicated to the data subject in clear and plain language. Silence, pre-ticked boxes or inactivity[5] do not meet the consent requirements under the GDPR as data controllers must ensure that there is a clear affirmative action, i.e. that the data subject has opted-in to the processing of their personal data. It also must be as easy for the data subject to withdraw their consent as it was to give it. A data controller is expected to maintain a record of consent, including who has consented or withdrawn their consent, when, how, and what they were advised. There are further special provisions for consent in relation to children, and as an applicant may be subject to additional requirements in relation to the processing of children's personal data (depending on the jurisdiction(s) of the processing), the applicant should be aware of these

---

[5] Recital 32 of the GDPR.

requirements and document how they are meeting them.

ii. The processing of personal data is necessary for the performance of a contract (to which the data subject is a party) or to enter into such a contract. Some examples of when this lawful basis could be used would be the processing of personal data required to enter into, or maintain, the contract between an employer and an employee or an individual's contract with their bank for a loan, or an individual's contract with an insurance company for their car insurance policy.

iii. The processing of personal data is necessary for compliance with a legal obligation that the data controller is required to meet. For example, the collection of personal data of employees by an entity for tax purposes, such as an employee's National Insurance number (sometimes referred to as a social security number).

iv. The processing of personal data is necessary to protect the vital interests of the data subject, or another living person. An example would be the processing of personal data in a life-or-death scenario, such as where there is an urgent need to access a doctor's medical file and the data subject/living individual is unconscious and therefore cannot give their consent.

v. The processing of personal data is *"… necessary for the performance of a task carried out in the public interest or in the exercise of official authority vested in the controller".* Consider the processing of personal data by a local authority to collect tax or the gathering of personal data as part of the country's census – this type of processing of personal data would fall under this fifth lawful basis.

vi. The processing of personal data is *"... necessary for the purposes of the legitimate interests pursued by the data controller or a third party, except where such interests are overridden by the interests of fundamental rights and freedoms of the data subject which require protection of personal data, in particular where the data subject is a child".* Essentially, it is lawful to carry out any reasonable processing once the processing is in line with the entity's interests or the interests of third parties. However, caution should be exercised to ensure that the interests, rights or freedoms of the data subject are not threatened and therefore entities relying on this lawful basis should carry out a legitimate interest assessment. Such an assessment should determine the purpose of the processing, how necessary the processing is, and the impact of the processing on an individual's interests and rights and freedoms.

The Europrivacy-certified certification body will assess the applicant's ToE to ensure that one of the above lawful bases can be applied to each of the applicant's specified data processing activities, and evaluate how the applicant is adhering to the lawful basis requirements. The certification body will also review the applicant's policies, procedures and records, through observation, interview and documentation review, to ensure that the applicant can demonstrate adherence to the requirements of Core Criteria 1.

Core Criteria 2: Special data processing

Core Criteria 1 focuses on the processing of personal data, but what about when an entity is processing more sensitive personal data or, as it is referred to in the GDPR, special categories of personal data?[6] Core Criteria 2 focuses on this type of data (e.g. personal data in relation to health, ethnicity, genetics, sexual orientation, etc.). This type of processing is prohibited except in very specific circumstances AND where one of the Core Criteria 1 lawful bases can be applied.

There are ten specific circumstances, outlined in Article 9 of the GDPR, permitting the processing of special categories of persona data. While we look at each of these ten in more detail below, it is imperative to keep in mind that a lawful basis AND one of the below circumstances are required to process sensitive data. The ten circumstances are as follows[7]:

i. *"The data subject has given explicit consent to the processing of those personal data for one or more specified purposes ... "*. This circumstance contains all

---

[6] Article 9 of the GDPR.

[7] Article 9(2) of the GDPR.

the consent requirements that are applicable under the lawful basis of consent for processing personal data, as discussed under Core Criteria 1, so explicit consent requires an affirmative action; it must be freely given, specific, informed, unambiguous and communicated to the data subject in clear and plain language; and it must be as easy to withdraw consent as it was to give it.

ii. The *"processing of special categories of personal data is necessary for the purposes of carrying out the obligations, and exercising specific rights, of the controller or of the data subject in the field of employment and social security and social protection law ... "*. This processing is permitted providing that it is authorised by law or by a collective agreement.

iii. The processing of special categories of personal data is *"... necessary to protect the vital interests of the data subject or of another natural person where the data subject is physically or legally incapable of giving consent"*.

iv. The processing of special categories of personal data *"... is carried out in the course of the entity's legitimate activities with appropriate safeguards, by a foundation, association or any other not-for-profit body with a political, philosophical, religious or trade-union aim"*. However, there is a caveat: the processing must relate solely to the members or to former members of the body or to persons who have regular contact with it in connection with its purposes, and the personal data must not be disclosed outside that body without the consent of the data subjects.

v. The processing of special categories of personal data *"... relates to personal data which are manifestly made public by the data subject"*. For example, if a data subject has published their sensitive data on a publicly accessible social forum or on the Internet, there is no requirement to obtain consent to process data that has already been manifestly made public.

vi. The processing of special categories of personal data is *"... necessary for the establishment, exercise or defence of legal claims or whenever courts are acting in their judicial capacity"*.

vii. The processing of special categories of personal data is *"... necessary for reasons of substantial public interest on the basis of Union or Member State law which shall be proportionate to the aim pursued, respect the essence of the right to data protection and provide for suitable and specific measures to safeguard the fundamental rights and the interests of the data subject"*.

viii. The processing of special categories of personal data is *"... necessary for the purposes of preventive or occupational medicine, for the assessment of the working capacity of the employee, medical diagnosis, the provision of health or social care or treatment or the management of health or social care systems and services ... ".*

ix. The processing of special categories of personal data is *"... necessary for reasons of public interest in the area of public health, such as protecting against serious cross-border threats to health or ensuring high standards of quality and safety of healthcare and of medicinal products or medical devices ... ".*

x. The processing of special categories of personal data is *"... necessary for archiving purposes in the public interest, scientific or historical research purposes or statistical purposes ... ".*

For numbers 2 and 7 to 10 of the above circumstances, there is an additional requirement that the processing must be on the basis of law, which must be proportionate to the purpose of the processing, must respect the data subject's right to data protection, and must provide for suitable and specific measures to safeguard the fundamental rights and interests of the data subject.

The GDPR includes a derogation[8] that permits EU member states to vary the definition of a special category, which means that some members states might include other types of data within its definition of sensitive or special categories of personal data. Therefore, an applicant must check its processing activities against all applicable special categories of personal data, depending on the jurisdiction it is based in or processing the data from.

---

[8] Article 9(4) of the GDPR.

In addition to the above circumstances for processing special categories of personal data, it would be remiss not to take into account any processing of data relating to criminal convictions and offences. The GDPR prohibits the processing of personal data relating to criminal convictions and offences unless the processing is carried out under the control of an official authority or the processing has been authorised by law. Therefore, if an applicant is processing personal data relating to criminal convictions and offences, it must ensure it has a basis for this processing as outlined in law.

The Europrivacy-certified certification body will assess the applicant's ToE to ensure that one of the above lawful bases from Core Criteria 1 and at least one of the circumstances listed above can be applied to any special category of personal data processing within scope of the certification. The certification body will also review the applicant's policies, procedures and records, through observation, interview and documentation review, to ensure that the applicant can demonstrate adherence to the requirements of Core Criteria 2.

Core Criteria 3: Rights of the data subjects

Chapter III of the GDPR outlines the eight rights that a data subject has in relation to the processing and protection of their personal data. Before we delve into each of these rights in more detail, this is a good time to mention the data protection principles as provided in Article 5(1) of the GDPR. They are as follows:

- Personal data must be processed lawfully, fairly and in a transparent manner.

- Personal data must be collected for specified, explicit and legitimate purposes.
- The processing of personal data must be adequate, relevant and limited to what is necessary for the purposes for which it was gathered.
- Personal data must be accurate and, where necessary, kept up to date.
- Personal data must not be stored for longer than is necessary.
- Personal data must be processed in a manner that ensures appropriate security.

Article 5(2) states that the controller must be responsible for, and be able to demonstrate compliance with, each of the above six principles. This requirement to be able to demonstrate compliance is known as the seventh data protection principle, i.e. the accountability principle.

The data subject rights link in with the seven data protection principles, as you will see when we go through each right in turn:

i. The right to be informed. The GDPR is specific about what information needs to be given to the data subject when collecting their data and how this information should be communicated to the data subject. In particular, there is a requirement to ensure that any communication to a data subject should be made in a concise, transparent, intelligible and easily accessible form, using clear and plain language that the data subject can understand.[9]

The GDPR very clearly lays out what information should be communicated to the data subject in Articles 13 and 14. Article 13 lists the information that must be provided to the data subject when the personal data is being collected from the data subject themselves, whereas Article 14 lists the information that must be provided to the data subject when the personal data has been obtained from a source other than the data subject.

Under Article 13, the list of information to be provided includes items such as:

- The identity and contact details of the controller and, where applicable, the controller's representative and DPO;
- The purpose of the processing and the legal basis for the processing;
- The legitimate interest of the controller or third party;
- The categories of personal data being processed;
- Any recipient or categories of recipients of the personal data;
- Details in relation to transfers of personal data;
- The retention period or the criteria used to determine the retention period; and
- The existence of data subject rights, etc.

---

[9] Article 12(1) of the GDPR.

Please refer to Article 13 of the GDPR for the full list of items to be included.

Article 14 specifies what information needs to be provided to the data subject when the personal data has been obtained from sources other than the data subject themselves. Where organisations buy lists from other companies, or personal data has come into an organisation through another channel, specific information must be communicated to the data subject in line with Article 14. The information to be provided is largely the same as when collecting information directly from the data subject, with one key addition: the data subject needs to be told where the controller got the data and if it was a publicly accessible source.

The most widely used method for providing all this information is via a privacy notice, which can normally be found on the homepage of an organisation's website.

ii. The right of access. Article 15 of the GDPR sets out the right of access that a data subject has, which essentially has three parts:
- The right to receive confirmation of personal data processing.
- The right to receive further information about how their data is processed (e.g. purposes of processing, recipients of data, sources of data, etc.).
- The right to access information about them that is being processed and/or to receive a copy of such information.

An access request is frequently referred to as a data subject access request (DSAR) or subject access request (SAR).

It is extremely important that data relating to third parties is not provided to the data subject as part of fulfilling the request, as this would constitute a data breach. Therefore, an entity must have a strong redaction process in place that is carried out before any data is provided to the data subject.

Under the GDPR, organisations have one calendar month to respond to an access request. While this appears to be an adequate time frame, if an organisation has an individual's data stored in multiple locations, across different systems or applications, and processes large amounts of personal data, this month could pass quickly.

iii. The right to rectification. This right is fairly self-explanatory – a data subject has a right to have their personal data corrected if it is incorrect, or completed if it is incomplete. This right overlaps with the principle that controllers must ensure personal data is accurate and up to date.

iv. The right to erasure. This right is also known as the 'right to be forgotten'. It is not an absolute right – there are specific circumstances in which it can and cannot apply. For example, this right applies in the following instances:

- The data no longer needs to be processed for the original purpose for which it was gathered.

- The data subject withdraws the consent on which the processing is based and there is no other legal ground for the processing.
- The data subject objects to the processing and there are no overriding legitimate grounds for the processing.
- The personal data has been unlawfully processed.
- There is a legal obligation in place requiring the data to be erased after a certain period.
- The personal data has been collected in relation to the offer of information society services.

It is important to note that if the applicant has disclosed information to any third parties, they will need to also inform these third parties about the erasure request.

v. The right to restriction. A data subject can request that the processing of their personal data is restricted. This means the data controller and data processor cannot continue to process the personal data until the restriction has been lifted. The only type of processing that can be carried out is that of storage, i.e. storing the personal data, which, as per the definition of personal data[10], is considered data processing. A data subject may invoke their right to restriction if:

- The accuracy of the data is contested;

---

[10] Article 4(2) of the GDPR.

- The processing is unlawful, and the data subject opposes the erasure of the personal data, requesting the restriction of it instead;
- The controller no longer needs the personal data for the purposes of the original processing, but the data is required by the data subject for the establishment, exercise or defence of legal claims; or
- The data subject has objected to processing pending the verification of whether the legitimate grounds of the controller override those of the data subject.

    Similar to the right to erasure, it is important to note that if the applicant has disclosed information to any third parties, they will need to also inform these third parties about the restriction on the processing of the personal data.

vi. The right to data portability. This means that data subjects have the right to obtain and reuse their personal data for their own purposes across different services and allows them to move, copy or transfer personal data easily from one environment to another in a safe and secure way.

    This right only applies to personal data that was provided by the data subject – it does not apply to any subsequent personal data that may have been derived during the relationship between the controller and data subject. This is the key difference between the right to data portability and the right of access.

vii. The right to object. This right effectively allows individuals to ask you to stop processing their personal data. It only applies in certain circumstances.

Individuals have the absolute right to object to the processing of their personal data if it is for direct marketing purposes.

viii. The right to object to automated decision-making, including profiling. This right does not apply if:

- The processing is necessary for entering into, or performance of, a contract between data subject and controller;
- The processing has been authorised by member state law that includes measures to safeguard the data subject's rights; or
- The processing is based on explicit consent.

Therefore, organisations need to ensure that the individuals are able to obtain human intervention in the decision making, express their point of view, and obtain an explanation of the decision and how they may challenge it. Where relevant, this explanation should obviously be included in the applicant's privacy notices at the point of collection.

Keeping the accountability principle in mind while facilitating a data subject request would mean that an entity should be maintaining a log of requests received, date received, date responded, any observations from fulfilling the request, etc.

An applicant's adherence to the accountability principle is thoroughly assessed during a Europrivacy audit, in that the applicant must be able to demonstrate their compliance with all applicable Europrivacy requirements. The certification body will also review the applicant's policies, procedures and records, through observation, interview and documentation review, to ensure that the applicant can demonstrate adherence to the requirements of Core Criteria 3.

Core Criteria 4: Data controller responsibility

When looking at the data processing activity, organisations will need to determine whether they are a data controller or a data processor. There are key differences between these two roles and the GDPR provides a definition of both, which will help applicants determine if they are acting as a data controller or data processor for each processing activity that they are seeking Europrivacy certification for:

- A data controller is a natural or legal person, public authority, agency or other body which, alone or jointly with others, determines the purposes and means of the processing of personal data.[11]
- A data processor is a natural or legal person, public authority, agency or other body which processes personal data on behalf of the controller.[12]

---

[11] Article 4(7) of the GDPR.

[12] Article 7(8) of the GDPR.

If an organisation determines that it is a data controller, then it needs to understand what the requirements are for data controllers under the GDPR with respect to processing – for example, privacy by design, breach notification and data protection impact assessments (DPIAs).

As per Article 24 of the GDPR, there are three key responsibilities that a controller has:

1. A controller must implement appropriate technical and organisational measures. This refers to a framework of controls that enables an organisation to manage its data protection and information security risks in one integrated system. A good example of this is the ISO 27001 standard, which has a broad range of organisational, people, physical and technological information security controls that can be applied to an organisation as appropriate. Additional data protection controls can be implemented to effectively align an organisation with the GDPR. A personal information management system (PIMS) aligned with the GDPR, such as ISO 27701 or BS 10012, could be considered.

2. A controller must implement appropriate data protection policies. Controllers need to review the policies they have in place and ensure that they are updated on a regular basis. Supervisory authorities will expect to see specific core policies in place, such as an information security policy, a data protection policy, an access control policy, etc.

Controllers need to ensure that their policies are effective, signed off by senior management and adhered to throughout the organisation.

3. A controller may adhere to codes of conduct approved by a supervisory authority. Approved codes of conduct are another method by which controllers can help ensure proper management of their data protection and information security risks. These are being updated all the time, so it would be prudent to regularly check for updates on your supervisory authority's website.

The Europrivacy-certified certification body will assess the applicant's ToE to ensure that a data controller is meeting its obligations under the GDPR for the specified data processing activities within scope. The certification body will also review the applicant's policies, procedures and records, through observation, interview and documentation review, to ensure that the applicant can demonstrate adherence to the requirements of Core Criteria 4.

Core Criteria 5: Data processors (or sub-processors)

If an organisation determines that it is acting as a data processor for the processing activity it is seeking Europrivacy certification for, then it needs to meet the obligations of data processors under the GDPR – Articles 28 and 29 refer to data processors' responsibilities. These include the following:

- The data controller must only use data processors that can provide the necessary guarantees to implement appropriate technical and organisational measures to ensure compliance with the GDPR, and to ensure that the data processor will protect the rights and freedoms of the data subjects.

- There must be a contract, or other legal agreement, in place between the data controller and the data processor. This agreement must take into account specific clauses incorporating the following:
  o Personal data must only be processed on the documented instructions of the data controller.
  o People processing the personal data must maintain the confidentiality of the personal data. This is usually covered via the confidentiality clauses within the employee–employer contract within the data processor.
  o The data processor must ensure it is taking all necessary measures to secure and protect the personal data that it is processing on behalf of the data controller.
  o The data processor must not engage another processor without the prior written approval of the controller.
  o The data processor will assist the data controller with regard to the fulfilment of data subjects' rights.
  o The data processor will provide help as necessary to ensure that the data controller is fulfilling its obligations in relation to security of personal data,

notifications of data breaches and completion of DPIAs.

o Upon termination of the agreement between the data controller and data processor, and regardless of which party initiates termination, the personal data must be securely deleted or safely returned to the data controller – the data controller decides whether the personal data is to be deleted or returned.

o The data processor will help the data controller provide all information necessary for the data controller to be able to demonstrate its compliance with the GDPR.

• If a data processor engages another processor (i.e. a sub-processor), the same data protection obligations as set out in the legal agreement between the data controller and data processor must be imposed on the sub-processor via a similar legal agreement.

• A data controller can request that its data processor adheres to an approved code of conduct or approved certification scheme (such as Europrivacy). This is a good method that data processors can use to demonstrate their compliance with the appropriate technical and organisational measures as outlined in the GDPR.

An applicant would need to have procedures to meet all the above criteria, including having the appropriate written contracts/agreements between all relevant parties in place.

In addition, the record of processing activities (ROPA)[13] is a key document that a Europrivacy-certified certification body auditor will want to see. Article 30 requires most data controllers to retain a record of their data processing activities. This record needs to contain a specific set of information such that it is clear what data is being processed, where it is processed, how it is processed and why it is processed. Data processors are also required to keep a record of all processing carried out on behalf of a data controller. Remember that the definition of 'processing' is so wide that even organisations that solely store, erase or destroy personal data are considered to be processing it.

The Europrivacy-certified certification body will assess the applicant's ToE to ensure that a data processor is meeting its obligations under the GDPR for the specified data processing activities within scope. The certification body will also review the applicant's policies, procedures and records, through observation, interview and documentation review, to ensure that the applicant can demonstrate adherence to the requirements of Core Criteria 5. An applicant's contracts/agreements with controllers, processors and sub-processors will also likely be inspected.

Core Criteria 6: Security of processing and data protection by design

Article 32 of the GDPR contains the obligations that data controllers and data processors must adhere to in order to protect personal data and safeguard the processing of

---

[13] Article 30 of the GDPR.

personal data. Key to this article is the focus on implementing appropriate technical and organisational measures to ensure a level of security appropriate to the risk.[14] The GDPR proposes the following as appropriate measures:

- The use of pseudonymisation and encryption.
- Ensuring the ongoing confidentiality, integrity, availability and resilience of processing systems and services.
- The ability to restore the availability of and access to personal data in a timely manner should there be a disruptive event (e.g. business continuity).
- To have in place a process for regularly testing the effectiveness of the measures implemented.

As you can see, the GDPR does not provide a lot of specifics in relation to the appropriate technical and organisational measures that a data controller or data processor can implement; however, Europrivacy maintains a comprehensive list of complementary technical and organisational checks and controls that are applicable for specific data processing activities (we will look at these later).

In addition, an applicant certifying to ISO standards such as ISO 27001 and ISO 27701 would be able to demonstrate compliance with a considerable number of what could be considered appropriate technical and organisational measures.

---

[14] Article 32 of the GDPR.

The GDPR requires both data controllers and data processors to be able to demonstrate their accountability (i.e. the pseudo-seventh data protection principle). How well an organisation can do this will depend on how effectively it has embedded data protection by design and by default in its operations. Data protection by design and by default can be implemented by ensuring that the organisation processes only data necessary for each specific purpose and that personal data is not made accessible to an indefinite number of people without the data subject's intervention.

This obligation of data protection by design and by default applies not only to the amount of personal data collected but also to:

- **The extent of the processing** – organisations should be using the least intrusive means possible to process the personal data;
- **The period of storage** – this should be for the minimum time necessary; and
- **The accessibility to the data** – there should be robust access controls and an individual's level of access should be granted in accordance with their role in processing the personal data. Generally, ISO 27001-compliant organisations will use the principle of least privilege, i.e. a user only has access to specific data that is needed to fulfil their role.

The obligation of data protection by design and by default is to process in the least intrusive manner possible by limiting the amount and range of information collected and processed (i.e. data minimisation) as well as controlling the number of people who have access to the personal data.

The Europrivacy-certified certification body will assess the applicant's ToE to ensure that a data controller/data processor is meeting its obligations under the GDPR for the specified data processing activities within scope. The certification body will also review the applicant's policies, procedures and records, through observation, interview and documentation review, to ensure that the applicant can demonstrate adherence to the requirements of Core Criteria 6, as well as evaluate the applicant's methods of assessing data protection risk.

Core Criteria 7: Management of data breaches

The GDPR definition of a personal data breach can be found in the 'Terms and definitions' section of this book. You will note that it includes all manner of data breaches, from headline-grabbing cyber breaches to accidental deletion of personal data. It can include instances where personal data has been lost or destroyed unintentionally. Personal data breaches can easily be caused by natural events (e.g. flooding of a ground floor housing servers storing personal data).

Not all breaches cause a risk to the rights and freedoms of data subjects, but organisations need to consider how they can ensure that all data breaches are reported internally so that proper decisions are made, both about what to report and how to deal with issues that could quickly escalate. For instance, a bug in a software application today could be exploited by a criminal hacker tomorrow.

When a breach occurs, it is important that an organisation knows when and who to notify (Articles 33 and 34 of the GDPR). If an organisation is a data processor, the data breach must be reported to the data controller without undue delay. There is no exception – all personal data breaches must be reported to the data controller.

When a data controller becomes aware of a data breach (via a data processor or not), it must risk assess the breach. If there is unlikely to be a risk to the rights and freedoms of the data subject, then the breach does not need to be reported. The organisation should still log the breach to ensure it is meeting its accountability requirements.

If the organisation determines there is a risk, then it must notify the supervisory authority without undue delay, but no later than 72 hours. This time frame is not working hours, so if the data controller becomes aware of the breach at 3:00 pm on a Friday before a bank holiday weekend, it has until 3:00 pm on the bank holiday Monday to notify the supervisory authority.

If the data controller determines there is a high risk to the rights and freedoms of a data subject, then it needs to notify the data subject without undue delay.

As you would expect, having a strong data breach reporting process in place is critical. This is something that the Europrivacy-certified certification body auditor will assess. While the certification body will review the applicant's policies, procedures and records, through observation, interview and documentation review, to ensure that the applicant can demonstrate adherence to the requirements of Core Criteria 7, it is also likely to assess how staff were trained to identify and respond to data breaches, inspect the records from data breaches, evaluate the applicant's methods of assessing data breach risk, and investigate to determine what lessons were learned and process improvements made.

Core Criteria 8: Data protection impact assessment (DPIA)

A DPIA assesses the risk of harm or other negative impacts on data subjects so that they can be mitigated.[15]

Organisations should ensure that a DPIA is part of their risk assessment process regarding personal data and is in line with their data protection by design and by default strategies. Conducting a DPIA does nothing to protect the rights and freedoms of data subjects – an organisation must also take appropriate steps to minimise the risk of harm, so the outcomes from completed DPIAs must be acted upon.

While the data controller is responsible for ensuring that DPIAs are conducted, it is not a requirement that the data controller performs the DPIA itself. In many cases where processing has been contracted to a third party, it may be more sensible to have the data processor conduct it.

The GDPR requires DPIAs to be completed for technologies and processes that are likely to result in a high risk to the rights of data subjects. In addition, Article 35(4) of the GDPR states that supervisory authorities in each EU member state must publish a list of the kind of processing

---

[15] "3: The Regulation", in *EU GDPR – An international guide to compliance* by Alan Calder, *www.itgovernance.co.uk/shop/product/eu-gdpr-an-international-guide-to-compliance*.

operations that are likely to be high risk and therefore require a DPIA. The supervisory authorities in the EU (and the Information Commissioner's Office in the UK) have published the list of processing activities that warrant the completion of a DPIA.

The Europrivacy-certified certification body will review the applicant's policies, procedures and records, through observation, interview and documentation review, to ensure that the applicant can demonstrate adherence to the requirements of Core Criteria 8. As well as evaluating the applicant's methods of assessing DPIAs, the certification body will review completed DPIAs to ensure that all required elements have been captured, and will refer to the relevant supervisory authority's list of processing activities where completion of a DPIA is mandatory.

Core Criteria 9: Data protection officer (DPO)

Chapter 4 of the GDPR outlines the requirements in relation to the designation, position and tasks of the DPO. Article 37(1) states three conditions where the appointment of a DPO would be mandatory:

1. If the data is processed by a public authority or body, except for courts acting in their judicial capacity.
2. If the controller's or processor's core activities consist of processing operations that require regular and systematic monitoring of data subjects on a large scale.
3. If the controller's or processor's activities consist of processing large quantities of special categories of

data and personal data relating to criminal convictions and offences.

While organisations that do not meet any of the above conditions do not have to appoint a DPO, it is not unusual for an organisation to appoint a DPO regardless.

It is crucial to note that Europrivacy requires an applicant to have designated a DPO. The DPO can be internal and carry out other tasks (once there is no conflict of interest) or the DPO can be an external body.

In addition to reviewing the applicant's policies, procedures and records, through observation, interview and documentation review, to ensure that the applicant can demonstrate adherence to the requirements of Core Criteria 9, the Europrivacy-certified certification body will likely review the DPO's resume, contract, qualifications and training records.

Core Criteria 10: Transfer of personal data to third countries or international organisations

International transfers are only considered GDPR compliant if they adhere to the conditions set out in Chapter V of the Regulation, i.e. organisations must comply with the six data protection principles and at least one of the following four conditions:

1. The transfer must be based on an adequacy decision – a transfer may take place to a country that is deemed to have an adequate level of protection. Adequacy is not something a country can bestow upon itself – the country must apply to the European Commission and

succeed in the application process. The list of adequate countries is published in the Official Journal of the European Union.

2. The transfer must be subject to an appropriate safeguard – personal data can only be transferred to a third country where there are appropriate safeguards, enforceable data subject rights and legal remedies. These appropriate safeguards may be provided by:

   - A legally binding and enforceable instrument between public authorities or bodies;
   - Binding corporate rules in accordance with the GDPR;
   - Standard data protection clauses adopted by the European Commission;
   - Approved codes of conduct; or
   - Approved certification mechanisms.

3. There is a derogation in place for the transfer – for example, a lawful basis for the transfer of the personal data (not to be confused with having a lawful basis for the processing of personal data).

4. There is a compelling legitimate interest for the transfer – transfers applicable under this condition are one-off, or infrequent, transfers of personal data concerning relatively few individuals.

Organisations based outside the EU should pay special attention to rules for international transfers because they also apply to transfers undertaken once the data has left the EU. Article 44 states: *"the conditions laid down in this*

Chapter are complied with by the controller and processor, including for onward transfers of personal data". For example, if personal data is transferred from Spain to India under a standard contractual clause agreement, a transfer from the original recipient to another organisation in India (or in another third country) must also meet the GDPR conditions for transfers. Transfers of personal data into the EU are not bound by such requirements, but there may be local laws that require some equivalent and Europrivacy addresses such national legislation as part of the completion of the National Obligation Conformity Assessment Report (NOCAR).

The Europrivacy-certified certification body will review the applicant's policies, procedures and records, through observation, interview and documentation review, to ensure that the applicant can demonstrate adherence to the requirements of Core Criteria 10.

2. Complementary contextual checks and controls

The complementary contextual checks and controls checklist is used to assess the data protection requirements that are relevant, or applicable, to specific technologies and applications.

Complementary contextual checks and controls are clustered in various subsets applicable to specific technologies and application domains such as:

- Public websites
- Video cameras and audio monitoring
- Internet of Things deployments
- Smart cities

- Biometric, medical and health data
- Automated decision making
- Blockchain and distributed ledger technology
- Data anonymisation and pseudonymisation solutions
- Artificial intelligence and data analytics
- Work environment and relationship
- Financial and insurance services
- Connected vehicles
- Smart grid and metering

Similar to the GDPR core criteria checklist, this list is mandatory for each certification relevant to data processing in these areas.

To consider what a subset of controls would look like, let us take artificial intelligence from the above list as an example. The Europrivacy-certified certification body would expect to see a completed DPIA fully assessing the risk to the data subject, with any identified actions implemented. Communication with the data subject would also be required, so the auditor would likely review data protection notices and policies to assess what was communicated to the data subject, what the lawful basis is for the processing, and whether the data subject has been given the option to override any decision made by AI if it is likely to have a significant (possible legal) impact on the individual. The certification body will review the applicant's policies, procedures and records, through observation, interview and documentation review, to ensure that the applicant can demonstrate adherence to the requirements on the complementary contextual checks and controls checklist.

3. Technical and organisational checks and controls

Adequate technical and organisational measures are required to be in place to protect personal data and the processing of personal data.

These checks and controls cover requirements such as the following:

- **Core security requirements** – such as data access restriction requirements, data encryption requirements and other security measures including requirements in relation to backup recovery tests (must be held at least once a year), regular server updates, denial-of-service mitigation, fire and flood protection, firewalling with least privilege port policy, and updated antivirus.

- **Extended security requirements** – such as connectivity checks for internal access, crypto management, penetration tests (the applicant must ensure that penetration tests are performed on a yearly basis and after any significant change that may affect the security of the personal data processing) and monitoring (intrusion detection rules, procedures or mechanisms).

These technical and organisational measures are mandatory; however, if the ToE does not include any high-risk data processing, these technical and organisation measures can be replaced by an active ISO 27001 (or ISO 27701) certification providing that it covers the data processing detailed in the ToE.

4. National requirements

Every country has data protection laws that may add to the existing requirements an applicant has to comply with to meet its data protection responsibilities. The GDPR requires data controllers and data processors to comply with all relevant national data protection legislation.

To demonstrate compliance with these national data protection obligations, an applicant must ask a legal expert to complete the NOCAR.

Europrivacy provides national data protection obligations profiles for each EU country, listing the important national conditions that an applicant must adhere to. These profiles can be found under the resources section within the Europrivacy Community online forum. To illustrate what could be taken into account for the NOCAR as part of these country profiles, let us consider the following three countries:

1. **Ireland** – the NOCAR would be expected to contain reference to the Data Protection Act 2018, the ePrivacy Regulation, the EU Data Act, the list of data processing operations that warrant the completion of a DPIA, etc.
2. **France** – the NOCAR would be expected to contain reference to the French Data Protection Act, the ePrivacy Regulation, the EU Data Act, the list of data processing operations that warrant the completion of a DPIA, etc.
3. **Germany** – the NOCAR would be expected to contain reference to the Federal Data Protection Act, the

ePrivacy Regulation, the EU Data Act, the list of data processing operations that warrant the completion of a DPIA, etc.

CHAPTER 5: THE CERTIFICATION PROCESS

This section outlines two separate certification processes:

1. The certification process for data processing related to products, processes and services.
2. The certification process for data processing activities related to data protection management systems.

It should be noted that there is a large body of work that must be undertaken before either of these certification processes commence. We will discuss this later when outlining the preparation that must be undertaken before submitting an application to the relevant certification body.

Table 1: The Certification Process For Data Processing Related To Products, Processes And Services

Stage 1	Application	Stage 6	Report
Stage 2	Scope validation	Stage 7	Issuing of certification
Stage 3	Offer	Stage 8	Maintaining certification
Stage 4	Documentation review	Stage 9	Certification renewal
Stage 5	Assessment		

Stage 1 – An applicant submits its Europrivacy application to the relevant certification body. This application, as well as including the applicant's relevant contact details, specifies the scope and ToE that is to be the subject of the certification process. The applicant states the personal data processing activities it wishes to be certified and its role as either a data controller or a data processor.

Stage 2 – Scope validation is conducted as the certification body reviews the application details, taking into account the ToE. This may warrant some communication between the applicant and the certification body to ensure that the scope has been understood. As a result, the application may require revision.

The certification body will decide whether to accept or decline the application. If it declines the application, it must contact the applicant to explain its decision. Should the certification body accept the application, it must then prepare an offer.

Stage 3 – The offer provided by the certification body must detail the scope of certification, information on the certification process, all terms and conditions, cost estimates for provision of the certification and a confidentiality agreement. The offer itself will have an expiry date. Once the applicant has formally accepted the offer, the certification body will create an audit plan and both parties will agree on an audit start date.

Stage 4 – The certification body auditor[16] conducts a review of all relevant documentation to assess what

---

[16] 'Auditor' refers to lead auditor, auditor or the audit team.

documents are in place, any omissions or incomplete documents, noting observations and nonconformities for each document. Europrivacy auditors must use the comprehensive documentation checklist and policy and procedures checklist for this documentation review process.

The documentation checklist includes a listing of documents such as the DPO's resume, an organisation chart, the DPO statement of compliance, the completed NOCAR, etc. The policy and procedures checklist includes policies and procedures in relation to data subject rights, data subject requests, data processors, etc., as well as specific policies such as the data confidentiality policy, the data minimisation policy, the data access policy, the data breach policy, etc.

The documentation review can be conducted remotely by secure sharing of the documentation between the entity and the auditor(s). There may be some documentation that cannot be shared, such as that of a highly sensitive or confidential nature, which is only available on-site. In these cases, the certification body auditor will attend the entity's office(s) to view the physical documents.

Should any documentation be considered deficient, the certification body will inform the applicant. The subsequent assessment stage may need to be rescheduled.

Stage 5 – The assessment is conducted at this stage, which involves the certification body auditor(s) performing testing activities in line with the "Suggested Means of Verification" for each relevant checks and controls checklist to assess the compliance of the ToE.

There are a number of checks and controls checklists that are provided to each Europrivacy auditor for use at this stage. These include:

- An application and ToE checklist;
- A list of complementary contextual checks and controls;
- The GDPR Core Criteria checklist;
- The technical and organisational measures checks and controls checklist; and
- The complementary surveillance checks and controls checklist (must be used for surveillance audits and recertification audits).

The auditor may use sampling methods and technical tests to identify any vulnerabilities or nonconformities.

On-site assessments or audits may be required – this will depend on the entity's ToE and should be communicated to the applicant during the scope validation stage. On-site assessments are permitted to use remote access and monitoring technologies.

An audit plan for the assessment is required to be provided to the applicant at least two weeks before the scheduled assessment commencement date.

Stage 6 – As part of preparing the audit report, the auditor will assemble all audit evidence including results of sampling, tests, reviews, observations, interviews, documentation checks, findings noted in checklists, etc., all of which must be verifiable. The auditor evaluates this data to formulate the audit findings.

The auditor will then document their findings in an audit report, which is submitted for review within the certification body. Once the report has been reviewed, the certification body makes a formal decision on the certification, which can lead to:

- Granting certification;
- Refusing certification;
- Amending the scope of certification;
- Restoring certification;
- Pausing certification;
- Renewing certification; or
- Withdrawing certification.

The finalised audit report is provided to the applicant, stipulating how each requirement is met or not met. This report also provides an explanation for the formal decision.

If a certification is granted, restored or renewed, the application moves to the next stage where certification is issued. If a certification is refused, paused or withdrawn, or the scope requires amending, the applicant is advised as to the reasons. Once an applicant has addressed the nonconformities that led to a declination, they may reapply.

Stage 7 – Once the certification body has decided to issue the certification (and received validation from the national supervisory authority, if applicable), the certification documentation is prepared. This documentation will include:

- The name and address of the certified applicant;

- The name and identification of the data processing activities or ToE;
- The scope of the certification;
- The date the certification was granted;
- The expiration date of the certificate;
- The unique reference code on the certificate;
- The Europrivacy logo or mark of conformity;
- The certification scheme;
- The name and address of the certification body; and
- The details of the people who made the certification decision.

In addition, the Europrivacy certificate will be registered and published on the official online Europrivacy Certification Scheme Registry.

Stage 8 – Certification is issued on a three-year basis and the certification body will conduct a surveillance audit on an annual basis to ensure that the applicant is maintaining their compliance. The surveillance audit will include an assessment of internal audits and management reviews completed since the previous audit, actions taken to address previous audit findings, the effectiveness of existing controls and any changes to the data processing activities.

The certification body will have a list of checks and controls – the complementary surveillance checks and controls checklist – as provided by Europrivacy, that must be assessed.

Stage 9 – Certification renewal is required before the expiration date of the certificate. Applicants will be invited to renew their certification before the expiration date.

Table 2: The Certification Process For Data Processing Activities Related To Data Protection Management Systems

Stage 1	Application	Stage 8	Stage 2 assessment audit
Stage 2	Scope validation	Stage 9	Audit report
Stage 3	Offer	Stage 10	Applicant adaptation
Stage 4	Opening meeting	Stage 11	Report review
Stage 5	Stage 1 assessment audit	Stage 12	Issuing of certification
Stage 6	Stage 1 reporting	Stage 13	Maintaining certification
Stage 7	Adaptation	Stage 14	Certification renewal

Stage 1 – An applicant submits its Europrivacy application to the relevant certification body. This application, as well as including the applicant's relevant contact details, specifies the scope and ToE that is to be the subject of the certification process. The applicant states the personal data processing activities it wishes to be certified and its role as either a data controller or a data processor.

Stage 2 – Scope validation is conducted as the certification body reviews the application details, taking into account the ToE. This may warrant some communication between the applicant and the certification body to ensure that the scope has been understood. As a result, the application may require revision and a meeting may be organised by the certification body with the applicant to establish the scope.

The certification body will decide whether to accept or decline the application. If the certification body declines the application, it must contact the applicant to explain its decision. Should the certification body accept the application, it must then prepare an offer.

Stage 3 – The offer provided by the certification body must detail the scope of certification, information on the certification process, all terms and conditions, cost estimates for provision of the certification and a confidentiality agreement. The offer itself will have an expiry date. Once the applicant has formally accepted the offer, the certification body will create an audit plan and both parties will agree on a date and time for the opening meeting. An audit plan for the assessment must be provided to the applicant at least two weeks before the scheduled assessment start date.

Stage 4 – The opening meeting is conducted. Its purpose is to ensure that the applicant is aware of, and in agreement with, the audit process. The certification body outlines the audit process, confirms attendees and documentation required for the audit, agrees methods for sharing documentation securely, and confirms the on-site or off-site audit activities due to take place. The certification body will also advise attendees of the confidentiality policy and the communication policy, and will seek validation from the applicant for the scope and audit plan.

Stage 5 – The certification body begins the stage 1 assessment audit, conducting a review of all relevant documentation to assess what documents are in place, any omissions or incomplete documents, noting observations and nonconformities for each document. Europrivacy auditors must use the documentation checklist and policy and procedures checklist as part of this documentation review process.

The documentation review can be conducted remotely by secure sharing of the documentation between the entity and the auditor(s). There may be some documentation that cannot be shared, such as that of a highly sensitive or confidential nature, which is only available on-site. In these cases, the certification body auditor will attend the entity's office(s) to view the physical documents.

Should any documentation be considered deficient, the certification body will inform the applicant. The subsequent stage 2 assessment audit may need to be rescheduled.

Stage 6 – The certification body auditor clearly documents all findings in its stage 1 assessment audit report. This report is shared with the applicant and all identified nonconformities are discussed to ensure that the findings are correct and understood. Normally, these findings are discussed during a meeting (on-site or remotely) at the conclusion of the stage 1 assessment audit. The date of the stage 2 assessment audit is agreed upon.

Stage 7 – The applicant has a number of weeks to address any findings, concerns or opportunities for improvement that came to light during the stage 1 assessment audit.

Stage 8 – The stage 2 assessment audit is conducted, which involves the certification body auditor performing testing activities in line with the "Suggested Means of Verification" for each relevant checks and controls checklist to assess the compliance of the ToE.

There are a number of checks and controls checklists that are provided to each Europrivacy auditor for use during the audit assessment. These include:

- An application and ToE checklist;
- A list of complementary contextual checks and controls;
- The GDPR Core Criteria checklist;
- The technical and organisational measures checks and controls checklist; and
- The complementary surveillance checks and controls checklist (must be used for surveillance audits and recertification audits).

On-site assessments or audits may be required – this will depend on the entity's ToE and should be communicated to the applicant during the scope validation stage. On-site assessments are permitted to use remote access and monitoring technologies. The auditor may use sampling methods and technical tests to identify any vulnerabilities or nonconformities.

During this stage 2 assessment audit, the certification body will ascertain the performance of the applicant's data protection management system to meet the requirements of all its data protection regulations. The certification body will also assess the applicant's planning, performance evaluation and continual improvement processes, including internal audit and management review.

Stage 9 – As part of preparing the audit report, the auditor will assemble all audit evidence including results of sampling, tests, reviews, observations, interviews, documentation checks, findings noted in checklists, etc., all of which must be verifiable. The auditor evaluates this data to formulate the audit findings and create the report.

The certification body auditor clearly documents all findings in its stage 2 assessment audit report. This report is shared with the applicant and all identified nonconformities are discussed to ensure that the findings are correct and understood. Normally, these findings are discussed during a meeting (on-site or remotely) at the conclusion of the stage 2 assessment audit – often referred to as the audit closing meeting.

Europrivacy has defined seven criteria status codes, which must be used to document audit findings[17]:

---

[17] Source: Europrivacy Certification Scheme – Handbook for Auditors, Europrivacy.

Status Code	Meaning/Explanation
?	Missing information/Don't know
OK	Conformity: Requirement has been controlled and appears to be respected and no non-conformities have been identified
OK+	Good practice moving beyond simple conformity
Obs	Observation
Min NC	A minor non-conformity (non-critical) has been identified
Maj NC	A major non-conformity (critical) has been identified
NA	Control is not applicable for the targeted certification

Stage 10 – The applicant has a defined period to address any findings, concerns or opportunities for improvement that came to light during the stage 2 assessment audit, or items that had been identified during the stage 1 assessment audit but had not been addressed. A correction action plan must be completed for each nonconformity identified, with evidence provided. The certification body will then verify the correction action plan and inform the applicant if further evidence is required.

An applicant cannot be granted certification if there are any open major nonconformities or more than five open minor nonconformities. If the certification body believes the certification would be misleading for data subjects and/or third parties, then it will not provide the certification.

Stage 11 – The audit report is submitted for review within the certification body. Once the report has been reviewed, the certification body makes a formal decision on the certification, which can lead to:

- Granting certification;
- Refusing certification;
- Amending the scope of certification;
- Restoring certification;
- Pausing certification;
- Renewing certification; or
- Withdrawing certification.

The finalised audit report is provided to the applicant, stipulating how each requirement is met or not met. This report also provides an explanation for the formal decision.

If certification is granted, restored or renewed, the application moves to the next stage where the certification is issued. If certification is refused, paused or withdrawn, or the scope requires amending, the applicant is advised as to the reasons. Once an applicant has addressed the nonconformities that led to a declination, they may reapply.

Stage 12 – Once the certification body has decided to issue the certification (and received validation from the national supervisory authority, if applicable), the certification documentation is prepared. This documentation will include:

- The name and address of the certified applicant;
- The name and identification of the data processing activities or ToE;
- The scope of the certification;
- The date the certification was granted;
- The expiration date of the certificate;
- The unique reference code on the certificate;
- The Europrivacy logo or mark of conformity;
- The certification scheme;
- The name and address of the certification body; and
- The details of the people who made the certification decision.

In addition, the Europrivacy certificate will be registered and published on the official online Europrivacy Certification Scheme Registry.

Stage 13 – Certification is issued on a three-year basis and the certification body will conduct a surveillance audit on an annual basis to ensure that the applicant is maintaining their compliance. The surveillance audit will include an assessment of internal audits and management reviews completed since the previous audit, actions taken to address previous audit findings, the effectiveness of existing controls and any changes to the data processing activities.

The certification body will have a list of checks and controls – the complementary surveillance checks and controls checklist – as provided by Europrivacy, that must be assessed.

Stage 14 – Certification renewal is required before the expiration date of the certificate. Applicants will be invited to apply to renew their certification before the expiration date.

Recertification may require a stage 1 assessment audit to be carried out, particularly in instances where there have been significant changes to the data protection management system, the applicant or the scope of certification.

CHAPTER 6: TERMS AND DEFINITIONS

- The *General Data Protection Regulation (the GDPR)* is a European Union data privacy regulation that took effect in every EU member state in May 2018.
- The *European Data Protection Board (EDPB)* is an independent body that brings together the national data protection authorities from across the European Union.[18]
- A *national data protection authority*, also referred to as a *supervisory authority*, is an independent public authority responsible for ensuring that personal data processing activities comply with all relevant legislation to protect the rights and freedoms of data subjects in relation to the processing and protection of their personal data.
- A *data subject* is the identified, or identifiable, natural person whose data is being processed.
- *Personal data* means *"any information relating to an identified or identifiable natural person ('data subject'); an identifiable natural person is one who can be identified, directly or indirectly, in particular by reference to an identifier such as a name, an*

---

[18] *https://edpb.europa.eu/about-edpb/who-we-are/european-data-protection-board_en*.

identification number, location data, an online identifier or to one or more factors specific to the physical, physiological, genetic, mental, economic, cultural or social identity of that natural person".[19]

- **Sensitive data** or **special categories of personal data** is *"personal data revealing racial or ethnic origin, political opinions, religious or philosophical beliefs, or trade-union membership, and the processing of genetic data, biometric data for the purpose of uniquely identifying a natural person, data concerning health or data concerning a natural person's sex life or sexual orientation"*.[20]

- **Processing of personal data** means *"any operation or set of operations which is performed on personal data or on sets of personal data, whether or not by automated means, such as collection, recording, organisation, structuring, storage, adaptation or alteration, retrieval, consultation, use, disclosure by transmission, dissemination or otherwise making available, alignment or combination, restriction, erasure or destruction"*.[21]

- **Pseudonymisation** means *"the processing of personal data in such a manner that the personal data can no*

---

[19] Article 4(1) of the GDPR.

[20] Article 9(1) of the GDPR.

[21] Article 4(2) of the GDPR.

longer be attributed to a specific data subject without the use of additional information, provided that such additional information is kept separately and is subject to technical and organisational measures to ensure that the personal data are not attributed to an identified or identifiable natural person".[22]

- **Encryption** is the *"security method of encoding data from plaintext to ciphertext, which can only be decrypted by the user with the encryption key".*[23]

- The **scheme owner** for the Europrivacy certification is the European Centre for Certification and Privacy (ECCP). It is the entity that has responsibility for maintaining, and developing, the Europrivacy certification.

- A **data controller** means *"the natural or legal person, public authority, agency or other body which, alone or jointly with others, determines the purposes and means of the processing of personal data".*[24]

- A **data processor** means *"a natural or legal person, public authority, agency or other body which processes personal data on behalf of the controller".*[25]

---

[22] Article 4(5) of the GDPR.

[23] *https://www.ibm.com/topics/encryption*.

[24] Article 4(7) of the GDPR.

[25] Article 4(8) of the GDPR.

- An entity that seeks certification is referred to as **the applicant**. The applicant must be either the data processor or data controller for the data processing activity that is the ToE.
- The **Target of Evaluation (ToE)** specifies the processing activities to be certified, so an entity's ToE will contain all personal data processing activities that are within the scope of the certification for that entity.
- **ISO 27001** is the internationally recognised standard for implementing and maintaining an entity's information security management system.
- **ISO/IEC 17065** details the requirements that bodies certifying products, processes and services must follow.
- **ISO/IEC 17021-1** contains *"principles and requirements for the competence, consistency and impartiality of bodies providing audit and certification of all types of management systems".*[26]
- A **consulting company** is an organisation that provides support services to an applicant – to identify any gaps in compliance, to help implement the requirements of the certification, to guide the entity through its preparation for certification and to support the entity in maintaining its compliance each year.

---

[26] *www.iso.org.*

- A Europrivacy *implementer* is responsible for helping entities implement the Europrivacy certification and also assists the entity in maintaining compliance with all applicable data privacy obligations. An implementer can be the entity's DPO or other individual within, or external to, the entity seeking certification. It is important to note that an implementer must be Europrivacy qualified – in other words, they must have passed the Europrivacy Introductory Course and the Implementer Course before they can deliver any Europrivacy services.

- *Certification bodies* are independent organisations that have been officially approved, by the relevant national data protection authority, as competent to carry out certification. Europrivacy provides a listing of qualified certification bodies on its website.[27] A qualified certification body is one that has received approval from Europrivacy to provide conformity assessments for the Europrivacy certification.

- A *Europrivacy auditor* is responsible for performing an audit against the requirements of the Europrivacy certification and delivering the audit report. To become a Europrivacy auditor, an individual must have passed the Europrivacy Introductory Course, the Implementer Course and the Auditor Course. The Europrivacy implementer cannot be the Europrivacy

---

[27] *www.europrivacy.org/en/partners/list.*

auditor for the same entity as there must be a level of independence observed with no conflict of interest. The Europrivacy auditor must have the expertise and skills required to perform the audit such as knowledge and understanding of the Europrivacy certification scheme, adequate expertise in data protection legislation as well as the necessary technical expertise so that they can effectively assess the technical and organisational measures within the certification scheme.

- *"A breach of security leading to the accidental or unlawful destruction, loss, alteration, unauthorised disclosure of, or access to, personal data transmitted, stored or otherwise processed"* is known as a ***personal data breach***.[28]

- A **third country** is any country outside of the European Economic Area (EEA), i.e. any country other than the EU member states and the three additional countries of Iceland, Liechtenstein and Norway.

---

[28] Article 4(12) of the GDPR.

FURTHER READING

IT Governance Publishing (ITGP) is the world's leading publisher for governance and compliance. Our industry-leading pocket guides, books and training resources are written by real-world practitioners and thought leaders. They are used globally by audiences of all levels, from students to C-suite executives.

Our high-quality publications cover all IT governance, risk and compliance frameworks and are available in a range of formats. This ensures our customers can access the information they need in the way they need it.

Other resources you may find useful include:

- *IT Governance – An international guide to data security and ISO 27001/ISO 27002, Eighth edition* by Alan Calder and Steve Watkins, *www.itgovernance.co.uk/shop/product/it-governance-an-international-guide-to-data-security-and-iso-27001iso-27002-eighth-edition*
- CyberComply, *www.itgovernance.co.uk/shop/product/cybercomply*
- Europrivacy Compliance Assessment, *www.itgovernance.co.uk/shop/product/europrivacy-compliance-assessment*

For more information on ITGP and branded publishing services, and to view our full list of publications, please visit *www.itgovernancepublishing.co.uk.*

To receive regular updates from ITGP, including information on new publications in your area(s) of interest, sign up for our newsletter at

www.itgovernancepublishing.co.uk/topic/newsletter.

Branded publishing

Through our branded publishing service, you can customise ITGP publications with your organisation's branding. Find out more at

www.itgovernancepublishing.co.uk/topic/branded-publishing-services.

Related services

ITGP is part of GRC International Group, which offers a comprehensive range of complementary products and services to help organisations meet their objectives.

For a full range of Europrivacy resources, please visit *www.itgovernance.co.uk/europrivacy.*

Training services

The IT Governance training programme is built on our extensive practical experience designing and implementing management systems based on ISO standards, best practice and regulations.

Our courses help attendees develop practical skills and comply with contractual and regulatory requirements. They also support career development via recognised qualifications.

Learn more about our training courses and view the full course catalogue at

www.itgovernance.co.uk/training.

Professional services and consultancy

We are a leading global consultancy of IT governance, risk management and compliance solutions. We advise organisations around the world on their most critical issues and present cost-saving and risk-reducing solutions based on international best practice and frameworks.

We offer a wide range of delivery methods to suit all budgets, timescales and preferred project approaches.

Find out how our consultancy services can help your organisation at

www.itgovernance.co.uk/consulting.

Industry news

Want to stay up to date with the latest developments and resources in the IT governance and compliance market? Subscribe to our Security Spotlight newsletter and we will send you mobile-friendly emails with fresh news and features about your preferred areas of interest, as well as unmissable offers and free resources to help you successfully start your project: *www.itgovernance.co.uk/security-spotlight-newsletter.*

Milton Keynes UK
Ingram Content Group UK Ltd.
UKHW051420050424
440540UK00010B/63

9 781787 785151